The Elephant

Illustrated by James Prunier
Created by Gallimard Jeunesse,
Claude Delafosse and James Prunier

MOONLIGHT PUBLISHING/FIRST DISCOVERY

The hairy mammoth,
a relative of the elephant,
lived thousands
of years ago.

Elephants
are the largest
mammals
living on land.

African elephants are bigger than Asian elephants.

Asian elephants have smaller ears and their heads are rounder.

Elephants live in Africa and in Asia.

Who is this old elephant?

She is the grandmother.
She looks after the herd
of females and
their young.

If the herd is threatened,
she will spread her ears to look fierce,
and charge the enemy,
giving the others time to get away!

Elephants usually have one baby at a time.
Very rarely, they have twins.

The baby grows
inside its mother
for 22 months.

The mother
helps the newly
born calf
to stand up.
Soon it is
suckling.

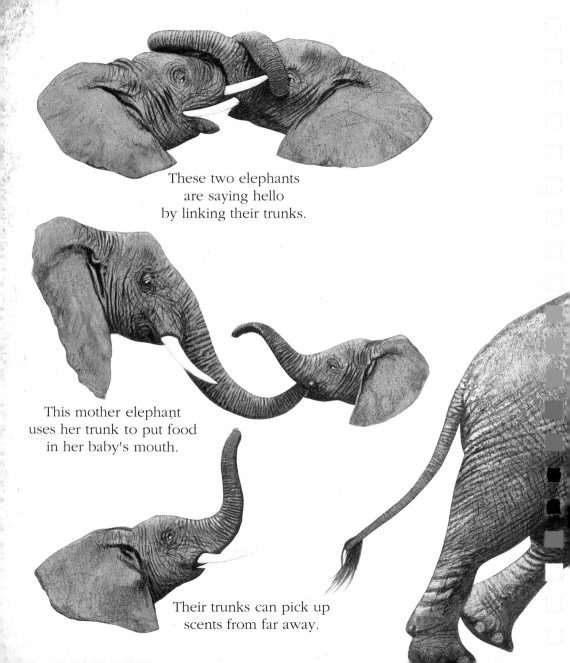

These two elephants
are saying hello
by linking their trunks.

This mother elephant
uses her trunk to put food
in her baby's mouth.

Their trunks can pick up
scents from far away.

There are so many things
an elephant can do
with its trunk.

Elephants use
their trunks to breathe,
to call or trumpet,
to pull off the branches
and bark they eat.

They drink...

...and they splash
themselves with their trunk...

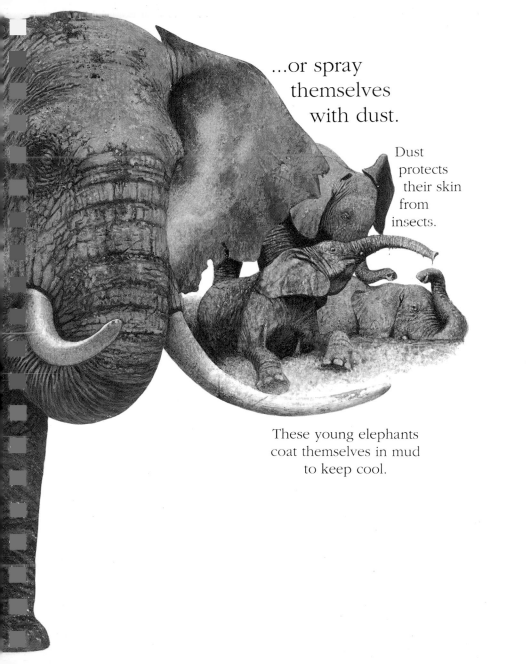

...or spray
themselves
with dust.

Dust
protects
their skin
from
insects.

These young elephants
coat themselves in mud
to keep cool.

Elephants live in
family groups which
often join together
to form large herds.

When an elephant is very old,
it will go away on its own
to die.

Adult males live together
in small groups.

In India
you can ride
on the back
of an elephant.

On feast days
the elephants
are dressed up
in all their finery.

An Asian elephant
will pick up, balance
and carry tree trunks.

They can push...

Asian elephants can be trained to work with men.

...or pull
very heavy
loads.

An elephant's tusks
are its incisors. They keep on
growing until the elephant
is very old, and then they wear away.

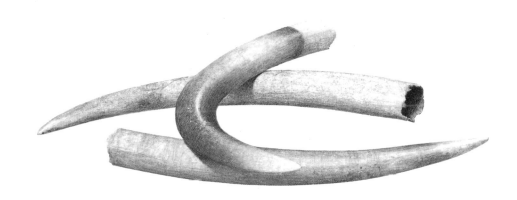

Elephants used to be killed for their tusks.
Ornaments and jewellery were made out of the ivory.
Nowadays people who hunt elephants
are severely punished.

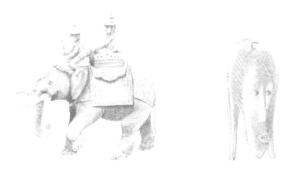

The elephant
is a gentle and intelligent giant
that should have to fear no-one.

Ostrich

Gazelle

Mouse

Giraffe

Look at these animals
that live in Africa.
Can you name them all?

Lion

Zebra

Chimpanzee

FIRST DISCOVERY: OVER 125 TITLES AVAILABLE IN 5 SERIES

American Indians
Animal Camouflage
Animals in Danger
Babies
Bears
The Beaver
The Bee
Being Born
Birds
Boats
The Body
The Building Site
The Butterfly
The Castle
Cathedrals
Cats
Christmas and New Year
Clothes and Costumes
Colours
Counting
The Crocodile
The Desert
Dinosaurs
Dogs
Ducks
The Eagle
Earth and Sky
The Earth's Surface
The Egg
The Elephant
Farm Animals
Finding a Mate
Firefighting
Flowers
Flying
Football
The Frog
Fruit
Growing Up
Halloween
The Hedgehog
Homes

The Horse
How the Body Works
The Internet
The Jungle
The Ladybird
Light
The Lion
Monkeys and Apes
Mountains
The Mouse
Music
On Wheels
The Owl
Penguins
Pictures
Pirates
Prehistoric People
Pyramids
Rabbits
The Riverbank
The Seashore
Shapes
Shops
Small Animals in the Home
Sport
The Story of Bread
The Telephone
The Tiger
Time
Town
Trains
The Tree
Under the Ground
Up and Down
Vegetables
Volcanoes
Water
The Weather
Whales
The Wind
The Wolf

FIRST DISCOVERY / ATLAS
Animal Atlas
Atlas of Animals in Danger
Atlas of Civilizations
Atlas of Countries
Atlas of the Earth
Atlas of France
Atlas of Islands
Atlas of Peoples
Atlas of Space
Plant Atlas

FIRST DISCOVERY / ART
Animals
Henri Matisse
The Impressionists
Landscapes
The Louvre
Pablo Picasso
Paintings
Paul Gauguin
Portraits
Sculpture
Vincent van Gogh

FIRST DISCOVERY / TORCHLIGHT
Let's look at Animals by Night
Let's look at Animals Underground
Let's look at Archimboldo's Portraits
Let's look at Castles
Let's look at Caves
Let's look at Dinosaurs
Let's look at Faires, Witches, Giants and Dragons
Let's look at Fish Underwater
Let's look at Life below the City
Let's look at Insects
Let's look at the Jungle
Let's look at the Sky
Let's look at the Zoo by Night
Let's look for Lost Treasure
Let's look inside the Body
Let's look inside Pyramids
Let's look for Lost Treasure

FIRST DISCOVERY CLOSE-UPS
Let's look at the Garden close up
Let's look at the Hedge close up
Let's look at the Oak close up
Let's look at the Pond close up
Let's look at the Rainforest close up
Let's look at the Seashore close up
Let's look at the Stream close up
Let's look at the Vegetable Garden close up
Let's Look under the Stone close up

Translator: Sarah Matthews - Editorial adviser: Laura Watkins and Andrea Ballard, WWF United Kingdom
ISBN 1 85103 146 4
© 1991 by Editions Gallimard Jeunesse

For Cécile

English text © 1992 by Moonlight Publishing Ltd
First published in the United Kingdom 1992
by Moonlight Publishing Limited, The King's Manor, East Hendred, Oxon. OX12 8JY
Printed in Italy by Editoriale Lloyd